THE WORKBOOK

ACCOUNTABILITY

IN THE WORKPLACE: WHY DOES IT MATTER?

DR. ANGELICA PIGMAN

Printed in the United States of America
First Printing, 2020

ISBN: 978-1-7354642-7-5

McWriting Publishing Services
Sharon Jenkins
2162 Spring Stuebner Rd
Suite#140-1018
Spring, TX 77389
Contact: sharon@mcwritingservices.com
Author Contact: pigman@classicapconsultant.com

CONTENTS

CONTENTS

CONTENTS

WELCOME!

Accountability Matters... to everyone! Yet sometimes we may wonder why it matters, especially in business. Accountability in the Workplace: Why Does it Matter? answers this question and a lot more. This book was written to promote building healthy accountability cultures in the workplace to alleviate the injustices that severely influence the business world and the communities that surround it.Dr. Angelica Pigman believes that accountability matters because employee performance sets the pace for a company's success in the marketplace. Accountability is also a major concern in the workplace because it affects the tangible outcomes of a business organization and it directly affects their bottom line.

No or limited productivity, no profitability!Accountability matters internally because it fosters respect, trust, and productivity in a company's business environment. It matters externally because it fosters customer satisfaction, builds brand loyalty, and establishes a company's industry foothold.In this book, it is our goal to thoroughly address the issue by defining the problem, suggesting viable solutions and reestablishing the importance of its consideration when mapping out business strategies for mission success in 21st Century

Regards,

Dr. Angelica Pigman

EMPLOYERS AND EMPLOYEES

CHAPTER ONE - WHAT IS ACCOUNTABILITY?

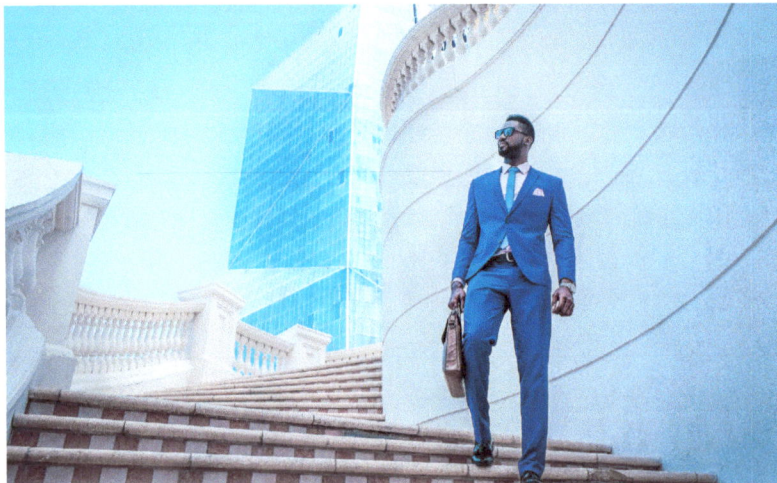

1 What does accountability mean to you?

2 How high does being accountability rank in your organization?

3 How does accountability work in your organization on an employee level?

4 What is the difference between accountability and responsibility?

5 Why does accountability matter to you?

6 How do you contribute to the accountability culture in your company?

CHAPTER ONE
FOUR KEY TAKEAWAYS

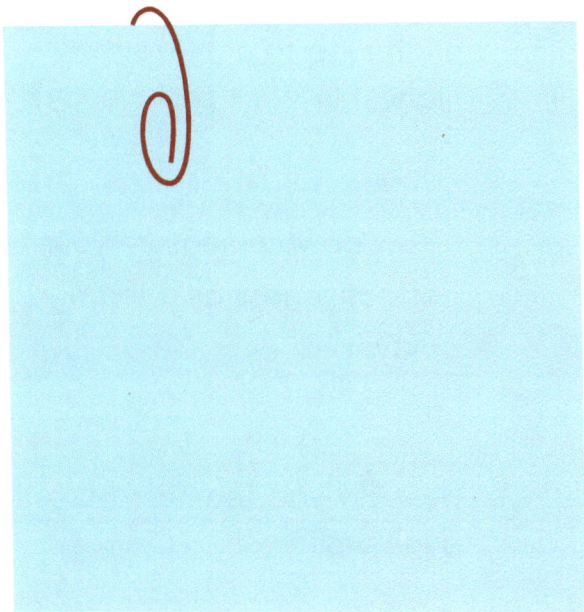

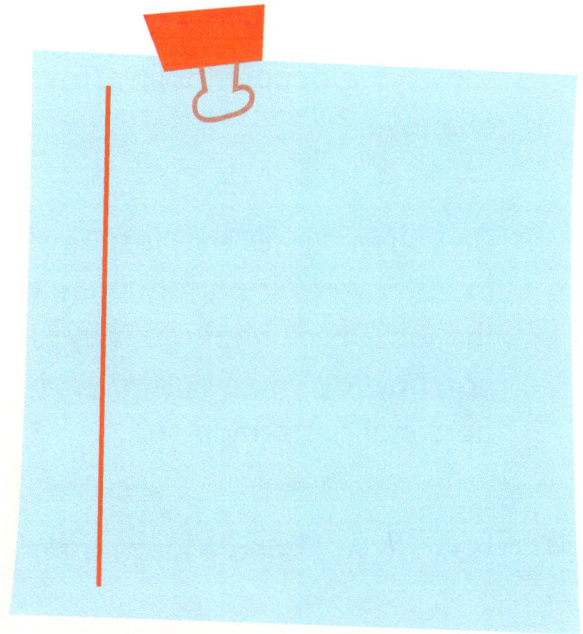

CHAPTER TWO - ACCOUNTABILITY FOR EMPLOYEES

1 What are the ways that you show your accountability to your employer?

2 Do you set goals that inspire you to improve your performance on the job? If so, what are they? If not, how do you measure your personal performamce?

3 How do you handle large tasks?

4 How do you manage your time on the job to achieve the highest level of proficiency?

5 How do you measure your effectiveness as a team player?

6 How do you reward yourself for a job well

CHAPTER TWO
FOUR KEY TAKEAWAYS

CHAPTER THREE - ACCOUNTABILITY AND MOTIVATION

1. What motivates you to go above and beyond the call of duty in the workplace?

2. What tangible incentives motivate you in the workplace?

3. What intangible incentives motivate you in the workplace?

4. Does your supervisor show appreciation for a job well done? If so, how? If not, why do you think this is the case?

5. How do you show appreciation for your employment opportunity?

6. Do you measure your value to your company by a consistent paycheck or the opportunity for promotion or to acquire more benefits?

CHAPTER THREE
FOUR KEY TAKEAWAYS

CHAPTER FOUR - ACCOUNTABILITY AND PERFORMANCE

EMPLOYERS

1. Do you know your employees' and their communications styles?

2. Do you have a plan/procedure to resolve employee conflict?

3. Are you a good listener?

EMPLOYEES

1. What is your communications style?

2. Are you proactive when dealing with workplace conflict? Are you aware of the company's policy and procedures concerning conflict?

3. Are you a good listener?

CHAPTER FOUR
FOUR KEY TAKEAWAYS

CHAPTER FIVE - ACCOUNTABILITY AND CULTURE

1. How are you assuming responsibility on the job in support of the overall company mission?

2. How do you contribute to building a healthy accountability workplace culture?

3. How do you foster comrade on the teams that you are assigned to work on?

4. Does your leadership [you, if you are a leader] cultivate accountability from ALL employees?

5. Are your leaders [you, if you are a leader] transparent, honest, and quick to assume responsibility for their [your] actions?

6. How are properly prioritizing your responsibility for building an accountability culture?

CHAPTER FIVE
FOUR KEY TAKEAWAYS

CHAPTER SIX – #ACCOUNTABILITYMATTERS

1 What key take away did you get from Chapter One

2 What key take away did you get from Chapter Two?

3 What key take away did you get from Chapter Three?

4 What key take away did you get from Chapter Four?

5 What key take away did you get from Chapter Five?

6 How will you contribute in the future to consistently build a positive accountability culture in the workplace?

CHAPTER SIX
FOUR KEY TAKEAWAYS

ACTIVITIES FOR EMPLOYEES

#ACCOUNTABILITYMATTERS GOAL-SETTING WORKSHEET

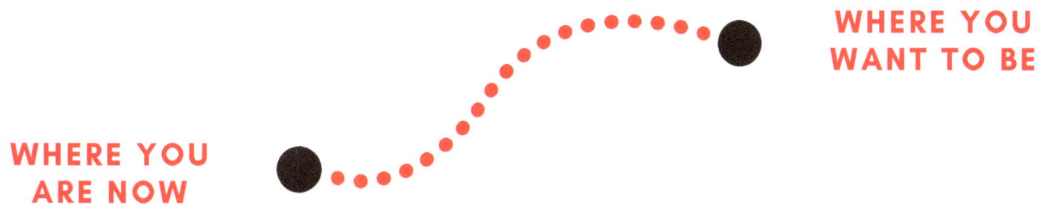

WHERE YOU ARE NOW

WHERE YOU WANT TO BE

01. Who is accountable for your success in the workplace?

02. Where does your accountability end and your employer's begin in your work environment?

03. How much time do you actually spend working during your workday? (Keep a log of your duties for a week and then calculate your actual time performing the duties outlined in your job description.)

#ACCOUNTABILITYMATTERS ASSESSMENT

01. On a scale of 1 to 10... How do you rate your work environment?

1 2 3 4 5 6 7 8 9 10

02. On a scale of 1 to 10... How do you rate the quality of your actual work experience?

1 2 3 4 5 6 7 8 9 10

03. On a scale of 1 to 10... How do you rate the compatibility of your education with your current work experience?

1 2 3 4 5 6 7 8 9 10

04. On a scale of 1 to 10... How do you rate your opportunity for advancement in this job assignment?

1 2 3 4 5 6 7 8 9 10

05. On a scale of 1 to 10... How do you rate your supervisor's support for task completion and your overall job success?

1 2 3 4 5 6 7 8 9 10

TOTAL: _____

WHAT YOUR SCORE MEANS

5 TO 20   If you scored within this range, there is a distinct need for accountability reassertion. It's time for a change, and taking this course is an excellent start.

21 TO 35   If you scored within this range, a regular team meeting (monthly or bi-monthly) would contribute significantly to raising the mastery of accountability in your workplace. Use this course as a point of discussion during those meetings.

36 TO 50   If you scored within this range, you are well on your way to an accountability culture that you can brag about. This course will confirm your excellence in the pursuit of an accountability friendly work environment.

MANAGEMENT

WORKPLACE STRATEGIES

Communicate the common purpose or "WHY" of your organization and why it matters in the industry, surrounding community, and to its internal and external customers.

Don't dictate, communicate clearly by relating clear and concise expectations. Define "WHAT" truce success looks like for the organization

Posture your company for success by positioning your team in alignment with a clear understanding of "HOW" everyone involved contributes to the overall mission of the company.

Establish a collaborative environment with checks and balances that indicate and monitor your progress. Make this information available to "EVERYONE."

Be transparent about all consequences, whether they are wins or loses; they matter to the team. Examining the "RESULTS" assists you in finding your naturally talented problem solvers and builds trust in your company.

ACTION ITEMS

- Make sure everyone understands the mission and vision of your company.
- Monitor communication between management and employees to eliminate the "blame game" message.
- Have FUN!

NOTES

_____
_____
_____
_____
_____
_____
_____
_____

#ACCOUNTABILITYMATTERS CHECKLIST

☐ **01. Are you getting to know your employees' personalities and understand their communication styles? Do you show your appreciation for their unique exceptionalities, skills, and talents? Are you cognizant of the favorite means of communication for your employees (internal customers)?**

☐ **02. Are you creating a receptive workplace environment? Are you a good listener? Do you work collaboratively with your employees to develop new employee policies and procedures?**

☐ **03. Do you offer comprehensive training when you are introducing a new process, product, service, software, or resource?**

☐ **04. Do you encourage feedback that accurately measures the effectiveness of your organization's policies and processes? When delivering constructive criticism, do you make sure that it is done privately and in a nonthreatening manner?**

☐ **05. Do you have a plan to resolve employee conflict quickly and make them aware of that process before its necessary to use it? Are you celebrating your employees and their successes, personal and professional?**

NOTES

YOUR ACCOUNTABILITY HABIT TRACKER

INSERT YOUR NEW ACCOUNTABILITY HABIT (GOAL) IN THE
APPROPRIATE ROUTINE. MONITOR YOUR SUCCESS BY CHECKING OFF ITS
COMPLETION EVERYDAY.

M   T   W   T   F   S   S

MORNING ROUTINE

_____

_____

_____

_____

_____

EVENING ROUTINE

_____

_____

_____

_____

_____

NOTES

DR. PIGMAN'S
#ACCOUNTABILITYMATTERS
PLANNING TOOLS

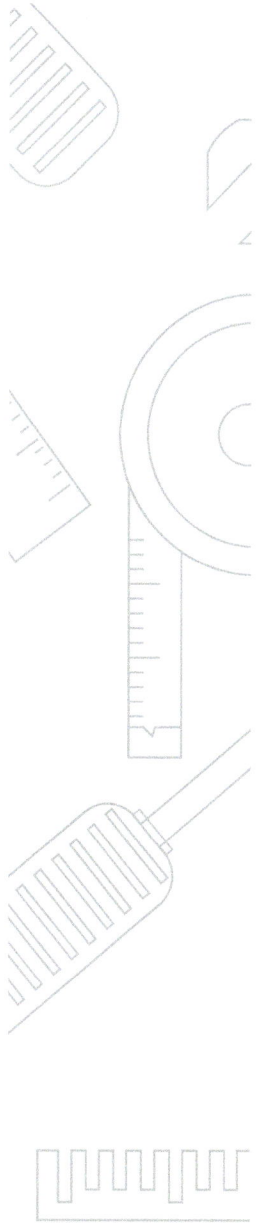

DISCOVER THE SUPERHEROS IN YOUR ORGANIZATION BY MAKING BUILDING AN ACCOUNTABILTY CULTURE AN INTERGRAL PART OF YOUR ORGANIZATION'S YEARLY AND QUARTERLY PLANNING PROCESS. HERE A FEW TOOLS TO GET YOU STARTED!

Dr. Angelica Pigman

YEARLY #ACCOUNTABILITYMATTERS PLANNER

YEAR:_____

JANUARY	FEBRUARY	MARCH
APRIL	MAY	JUNE
JULY	AUGUST	SEPTEMBER
OCTOBER	NOVEMBER	DECEMBER

90-DAY #ACCOUNTABILITYMATTERS PLANNER

GOAL #1	GOAL #2	GOAL #3

ACTION STEPS	ACTION STEPS	ACTION STEPS

NOTES

_____

_____

_____

_____

#ACCOUNTABILITYMATTERS
NOTES / BRAINSTORMING PAGE

#ACCOUTABILITYMATTERS TO-DO LIST

TASKS	PRIORITY	DUE DATE	
			☐
			☐
			☐
			☐
			☐
			☐
			☐
			☐
			☐
			☐
			☐
			☐
			☐
			☐
			☐
			☐
			☐
			☐
			☐
			☐

"

When your work speaks for itself, don't interrupt.

– HENRY J. KAISER

ABOUT THE AUTHOR

DR. ANGELICA PIGMAN

Angelica Pigman, DBA. is the founder and CEO of Classic AP Consultant. Dr. Angelica's mission is to teach others how to grow through faith and marketplace skills to enhance themselves and their business.

Dr. Pigman's journey began as a Provider Relations Advocate in the health care industry. She has logged nearly twenty years of experience in various areas of managed care (provider relations, retention account manager, quality improvement specialist, telephonic service coordinator and authorization coordinator).

In additional to her extensive experience, Dr. Angelica also has outstanding academic background that includes a Doctorate in Business Administration (Strategy & Innovation) from Capella University in Minnesota and a Masters in Business Management from Letourneau University in Houston. Dr. Angelica is also a Certified Life Coach from The Bloom Life Coach Institute.

Dr. Angelica's combination of academic qualifications, health care and coaching experience provides a strong foundation for the kind of work approach to business owners and helping others heal and thrive. The training she received from the Bloom Institute gave her a deep understanding of how we get stuck in negative patterns and settle for unfulfilled lives of mediocrity because we're disconnected from the full expression of our talents.

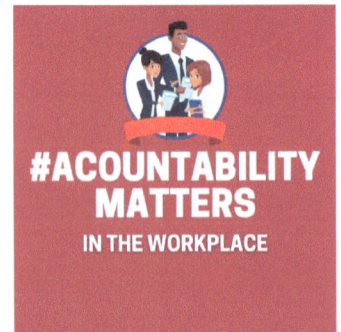

#ACOUNTABILITY MATTERS
IN THE WORKPLACE

READY FOR THE NEXT LEVEL?

I'm opening the doors to my exclusive
one-on-one coaching program for
high-performing female CEOs very soon.

And since you've completed my course,
I think you could be a perfect fit!

APPLY TO JOIN MY COACHING PROGRAM
PIGMAN@CLASSICAPCONSULTANT.COM

"THIS IS THE BEST INVESTMENT YOU CAN EVER
MAKE IS IN YOURSELF. THEN EVERYONE
PROSPERS WHEN YOU JOIN THEIR TEAM."

- Dr. Angelica Pigman

WANT TO TURN YOUR WORKPLACE PASSIONS INTO PROFITS?

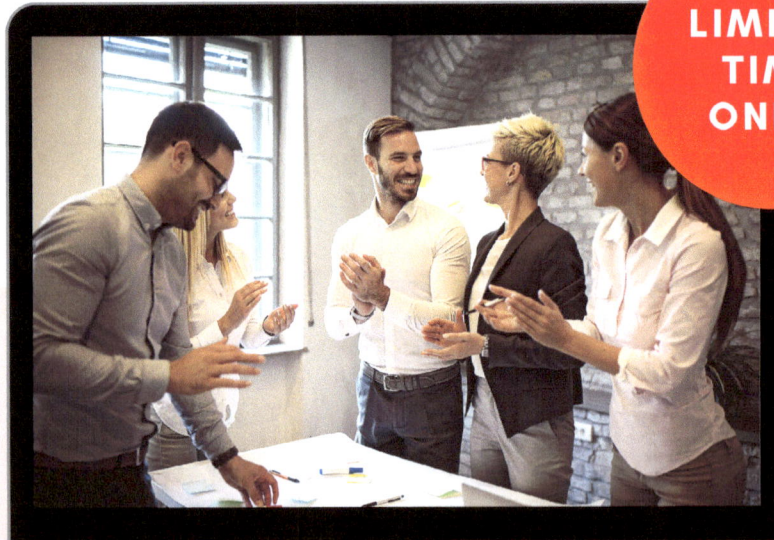

LIMITED TIME ONLY!

Join me on an exclusive masterclass where I share all my secrets on how to make an accountability culture profitable... even if you're starting from scratch!

REGISTER FOR THE EXCLUSIVE WEBINAR
PIGMAN@CLASSICAPCONSULTANT.COM

www.ingramcontent.com/pod-product-compliance
Lightning Source LLC
Chambersburg PA
CBHW052049190326
41521CB00002BA/155